GRATITUDE

JOURNAL

TINY HOOVES, STEADY HEART

PEANUT IS A MINIATURE HORSE AT **FOX LEA MINI HORSE RESCUE**. SHE WAS BORN AT THE RESCUE AFTER HER MOTHER WAS SAVED FROM A DISASTROUS SITUATION
.

SMALL IN SIZE BUT BIG IN HEART, PEANUT HAS BECOME THE RESCUE'S AMBASSADOR MINI, MEETING EVERY CHALLENGE WITH CHARM-FROM BUSY HORSE EXPOSITIONS TO THE QUIET COMFORT OF NURSING HOMES, AND FROM EXCITED DAYCARE VISITS TO CURIOUS PRESCHOOL CLASSROOMS.

THROUGH HER GENTLE SPIRIT AND TINY-HOOVED WISDOM, PEANUT HOPES THE ESSONS SHE SHARES WILL HELP OTHERS NOTICE THE FOOD, FIND COURAGE IN SMALL MOMENTS AND CARRY A STEADIER HEART.

THIS JOURNAL BELONGS TO:

____

Start the day with one small good thing

PEANUT

HOW TO USE THIS JOURNAL

This journal is meant to be a quiet place to pause, breathe, and notice the good that is already woven into your life. You do not need to write perfectly, think deeply every day, or have something profound to say. Like a mini horse standing peacefully in the morning light, this practice is about showing up gently and honestly.

Each page gives you a simple way to reflect on your day. In "Today I am grateful for,"write down anything that brought comfort, joy, relief, or peace.

The section "Three things that made me happy today" helps you notice small bright moments before they slip away. In "Today I learned," write down something the day taught you. In "A challenge I overcame," give yourself credit.

Finally, "One thing I can improve tomorrow" is not for criticism. It is simply a soft invitation to grow.

Use this journal in the morning, at night, or whenever your heart needs a little pasture space. There is no wrong way to begin.
Start with one small good thing, and let it lead you home.

Date:

**"START WITH ONE SMALL GOOD THING.
THE HEART KNOWS HOW TO GROW FROM THERE."**
PEANUT

TODAY I AM GRATEFUL FOR

I AM LOOKING FORWARD TO

THREE THINGS THAT MADE ME HAPPY TODAY

TODAY I LEARNED...

A CHALLENGE I OVERCAME

ONE THING I CAN IMPROVE TOMORROW

My Positive Affirmation for Today...

Date:

"IF YOU FOUND ONE GOOD THING TODAY, YOU FOUND A BEGINNING."

PEANUT

TODAY I AM GRATEFUL FOR

I AM LOOKING FORWARD TO

THREE THINGS THAT MADE ME HAPPY TODAY

TODAY I LEARNED...

A CHALLENGE I OVERCAME

ONE THING I CAN IMPROVE TOMORROW

My Positive Affirmation for Today...

Date:

“GRATITUDE DOES NOT MEAN THE DAY WAS EASY. IT MEANS SOMETHING SOFT STILL FOUND YOU.”.

PEANUT

TODAY I AM GRATEFUL FOR

I AM LOOKING FORWARD TO

THREE THINGS THAT MADE ME HAPPY TODAY

TODAY I LEARNED...

A CHALLENGE I OVERCAME

ONE THING I CAN IMPROVE TOMORROW

My Positive Affirmation for Today...

Date:

"WHEN YOU LOOK FOR WHAT IS GENTLE, THE WHOLE PASTURE CHANGES."

PEANUT

TODAY I AM GRATEFUL FOR

I AM LOOKING FORWARD TO

THREE THINGS THAT MADE ME HAPPY TODAY

TODAY I LEARNED...

A CHALLENGE I OVERCAME

ONE THING I CAN IMPROVE TOMORROW

My Positive Affirmation for Today...

Date:

"THE SMALLEST GOOD THING STILL COUNTS. TRUST ME, I AM A SMALL GOOD THING."

PEANUT

TODAY I AM GRATEFUL FOR

I AM LOOKING FORWARD TO

THREE THINGS THAT MADE ME HAPPY TODAY

TODAY I LEARNED...

A CHALLENGE I OVERCAME

ONE THING I CAN IMPROVE TOMORROW

My Positive Affirmation for Today...

Date:

"GRATITUDE IS NOTICING THE LITTLE THINGS BEFORE THEY BECOME THE BIG THINGS WE MISS."

PEANUT

TODAY I AM GRATEFUL FOR

I AM LOOKING FORWARD TO

THREE THINGS THAT MADE ME HAPPY TODAY

TODAY I LEARNED...

A CHALLENGE I OVERCAME

ONE THING I CAN IMPROVE TOMORROW

My Positive Affirmation for Today...

Date: ____________

"YOU CAN FIND JOY IN A SUNBEAM, A SNACK, AND SOMEONE WHO KNOWS YOUR NAME."
PEANUT

TODAY I AM GRATEFUL FOR

I AM LOOKING FORWARD TO

THREE THINGS THAT MADE ME HAPPY TODAY

TODAY I LEARNED...

A CHALLENGE I OVERCAME

ONE THING I CAN IMPROVE TOMORROW

My Positive Affirmation for Today...

Date:

"THE HEART GROWS STEADIER WHEN IT REMEMBERS WHAT STAYED."
PEANUT

TODAY I AM GRATEFUL FOR

I AM LOOKING FORWARD TO

THREE THINGS THAT MADE ME HAPPY TODAY

TODAY I LEARNED...

A CHALLENGE I OVERCAME

ONE THING I CAN IMPROVE TOMORROW

My Positive Affirmation for Today...

Date:

"SOME DAYS THE BLESSING
IS SIMPLY
MAKING IT SAFELY TO EVENING."
PEANUT

TODAY I AM GRATEFUL FOR

I AM LOOKING FORWARD TO

THREE THINGS THAT MADE ME HAPPY TODAY

TODAY I LEARNED...

A CHALLENGE I OVERCAME

ONE THING I CAN IMPROVE TOMORROW

My Positive Affirmation for Today...

Date: ______________________

"A WHOLE LIFE IS BUILT FROM 'NOWS' -ONE BREATH, ONE BLESSING, ONE HOOFSTEP AT A TIME."

PEANUT

TODAY I AM GRATEFUL FOR

I AM LOOKING FORWARD TO

THREE THINGS THAT MADE ME HAPPY TODAY

TODAY I LEARNED...

A CHALLENGE I OVERCAME

ONE THING I CAN IMPROVE TOMORROW

My Positive Affirmation for Today...

Date:

"A GRATEFUL HEART DOES NOT NEED A PERFECT PASTURE."
PEANUT

TODAY I AM GRATEFUL FOR

I AM LOOKING FORWARD TO

THREE THINGS THAT MADE ME HAPPY TODAY

TODAY I LEARNED...

A CHALLENGE I OVERCAME

ONE THING I CAN IMPROVE TOMORROW

My Positive Affirmation for Today...

Date:

"TURN YOUR NOSE TOWARD THE SUNSHINE, LET THE SHADOWS FALL BEHIND YOU."
PEANUT

TODAY I AM GRATEFUL FOR

I AM LOOKING FORWARD TO

THREE THINGS THAT MADE ME HAPPY TODAY

TODAY I LEARNED...

A CHALLENGE I OVERCAME

ONE THING I CAN IMPROVE TOMORROW

My Positive Affirmation for Today...

Date: ____________

"LET THE SMALL JOYS COUNT. THEY ARE DOING MORE THAN YOU KNOW."
PEANUT

TODAY I AM GRATEFUL FOR

I AM LOOKING FORWARD TO

THREE THINGS THAT MADE ME HAPPY TODAY

TODAY I LEARNED...

A CHALLENGE I OVERCAME

ONE THING I CAN IMPROVE TOMORROW

My Positive Affirmation for Today...

Date:

"I AM NOT PERFECT, BUT I AM STILL PRECIOUS."
PEANUT

TODAY I AM GRATEFUL FOR

I AM LOOKING FORWARD TO

THREE THINGS THAT MADE ME HAPPY TODAY

TODAY I LEARNED...

A CHALLENGE I OVERCAME

ONE THING I CAN IMPROVE TOMORROW

My Positive Affirmation for Today...

Date:

"A LITTLE HOPE IS STILL HOPE."
PEANUT

TODAY I AM GRATEFUL FOR

I AM LOOKING FORWARD TO

THREE THINGS THAT MADE ME HAPPY TODAY

TODAY I LEARNED...

A CHALLENGE I OVERCAME

ONE THING I CAN IMPROVE TOMORROW

My Positive Affirmation for Today...

Date:

"YOU DO NOT HAVE TO GALLOP YOU JUST HAVE TO START WALKING."

PEANUT

TODAY I AM GRATEFUL FOR

I AM LOOKING FORWARD TO

THREE THINGS THAT MADE ME HAPPY TODAY

TODAY I LEARNED...

A CHALLENGE I OVERCAME

ONE THING I CAN IMPROVE TOMORROW

My Positive Affirmation for Today...

Date:

"EVEN ON MUDDY DAYS,
THERE IS SOMETHING WORTH NOTICING."
PEANUT

TODAY I AM GRATEFUL FOR

I AM LOOKING FORWARD TO

THREE THINGS THAT MADE ME HAPPY TODAY

TODAY I LEARNED...

A CHALLENGE I OVERCAME

ONE THING I CAN IMPROVE TOMORROW

My Positive Affirmation for Today...

Date:

**"I AM NOT AFRAID OF STORMS.
I AM LEARNING
HOW TO STAND STEADY UNTIL THE SKY SOFTENS."**

PEANUT

TODAY I AM GRATEFUL FOR

I AM LOOKING FORWARD TO

THREE THINGS THAT MADE ME HAPPY TODAY

TODAY I LEARNED...

A CHALLENGE I OVERCAME

ONE THING I CAN IMPROVE TOMORROW

My Positive Affirmation for Today...

Date: ____________

“THE MORNING DOES NOT ASK YOU TO BE READY. IT ONLY ASKS YOU TO ARRIVE.”
PEANUT

TODAY I AM GRATEFUL FOR

I AM LOOKING FORWARD TO

THREE THINGS THAT MADE ME HAPPY TODAY

TODAY I LEARNED...

A CHALLENGE I OVERCAME

ONE THING I CAN IMPROVE TOMORROW

My Positive Affirmation for Today...

Date:

"KINDNESS IS FELT
BEFORE IT IS UNDERSTOOD."
PEANUT

TODAY I AM GRATEFUL FOR

I AM LOOKING FORWARD TO

THREE THINGS THAT MADE ME HAPPY TODAY

TODAY I LEARNED...

A CHALLENGE I OVERCAME

ONE THING I CAN IMPROVE TOMORROW

My Positive Affirmation for Today...

Date:

"LOOK FOR ONE SOFT MOMENT IN YOUR DAY."
PEANUT

TODAY I AM GRATEFUL FOR

I AM LOOKING FORWARD TO

THREE THINGS THAT MADE ME HAPPY TODAY

TODAY I LEARNED...

A CHALLENGE I OVERCAME

ONE THING I CAN IMPROVE TOMORROW

My Positive Affirmation for Today...

Date:

"SMALL KINDNESS STILL COUNTS.
TRUST ME,
SMALL THINGS CAN DO VERY BIG WORK.".

PEANUT

TODAY I AM GRATEFUL FOR

I AM LOOKING FORWARD TO

THREE THINGS THAT MADE ME HAPPY TODAY

TODAY I LEARNED...

A CHALLENGE I OVERCAME

ONE THING I CAN IMPROVE TOMORROW

My Positive Affirmation for Today...

Date:

**"YOU CAN BE TIRED
AND
THANKFUL
AT THE SAME TIME."**
PEANUT

TODAY I AM GRATEFUL FOR

I AM LOOKING FORWARD TO

THREE THINGS THAT MADE ME HAPPY TODAY

TODAY I LEARNED...

A CHALLENGE I OVERCAME

ONE THING I CAN IMPROVE TOMORROW

My Positive Affirmation for Today...

Date: ____________

"DESTINY IS NOT HIDING IN THE STARS IT BEGINS RIGHT UNDER YOUR TINY HOOVES."
PEANUT

TODAY I AM GRATEFUL FOR

I AM LOOKING FORWARD TO

THREE THINGS THAT MADE ME HAPPY TODAY

TODAY I LEARNED...

A CHALLENGE I OVERCAME

ONE THING I CAN IMPROVE TOMORROW

My Positive Affirmation for Today...

Date:

"THERE IS ALWAYS ROOM IN THE PASTURE FOR ONE MORE GRATEFUL THOUGHT."

PEANUT

TODAY I AM GRATEFUL FOR

I AM LOOKING FORWARD TO

THREE THINGS THAT MADE ME HAPPY TODAY

TODAY I LEARNED...

A CHALLENGE I OVERCAME

ONE THING I CAN IMPROVE TOMORROW

My Positive Affirmation for Today...

Date:

"NEVER DOUBT THE GLOW OF ONE LITTLE LIGHT. IT MAY BE EXACTLY WHAT SOMEONE NEEDS TO FIND THE GATE."

PEANUT

TODAY I AM GRATEFUL FOR

I AM LOOKING FORWARD TO

THREE THINGS THAT MADE ME HAPPY TODAY

TODAY I LEARNED...

A CHALLENGE I OVERCAME

ONE THING I CAN IMPROVE TOMORROW

My Positive Affirmation for Today...

Date:

"A MINI HORSE NEVER WAKES UP WONDERING IF SHE HAS EARNED BREAKFAST, REST, FRIENDSHIP, OR A SPACE IN THE PASTURE."

PEANUT

TODAY I AM GRATEFUL FOR

I AM LOOKING FORWARD TO

THREE THINGS THAT MADE ME HAPPY TODAY

TODAY I LEARNED...

A CHALLENGE I OVERCAME

ONE THING I CAN IMPROVE TOMORROW

My Positive Affirmation for Today...

Date: ____________

“WHEN IT RAINS, LET IT RAIN A WISE LITTLE HORSE KNOWS THE GRASS IS STILL GROWING.”
PEANUT

TODAY I AM GRATEFUL FOR

I AM LOOKING FORWARD TO

THREE THINGS THAT MADE ME HAPPY TODAY

TODAY I LEARNED...

A CHALLENGE I OVERCAME

ONE THING I CAN IMPROVE TOMORROW

My Positive Affirmation for Today...

Date:

**"NOT EVERY SEASON IS MEANT FOR SPEED.
SOME SEASONS ARE MEANT
FOR GROWING TRUST
AND STANDING IN THE SUN."**
PEANUT

TODAY I AM GRATEFUL FOR

I AM LOOKING FORWARD TO

THREE THINGS THAT MADE ME HAPPY TODAY

TODAY I LEARNED...

A CHALLENGE I OVERCAME

ONE THING I CAN IMPROVE TOMORROW

My Positive Affirmation for Today...

Date:

"A QUIET MOMENT CAN BE A VERY LARGE GIFT."
PEANUT

TODAY I AM GRATEFUL FOR

I AM LOOKING FORWARD TO

THREE THINGS THAT MADE ME HAPPY TODAY

TODAY I LEARNED...

A CHALLENGE I OVERCAME

ONE THING I CAN IMPROVE TOMORROW

My Positive Affirmation for Today...

Date: ____________

"SOME DAYS ARE FOR GRAZING QUIETLY, NOT PROVING YOURSELF."
PEANUT

TODAY I AM GRATEFUL FOR

I AM LOOKING FORWARD TO

THREE THINGS THAT MADE ME HAPPY TODAY

TODAY I LEARNED...

A CHALLENGE I OVERCAME

ONE THING I CAN IMPROVE TOMORROW

My Positive Affirmation for Today...

Date:

"SOMETIMES THE HERD DOES NOT NEED YOU TO FIX EVERYTHING. SOMETIMES THEY ONLY NEED YOU TO STAND BESIDE THEM CALMLY."

PEANUT

TODAY I AM GRATEFUL FOR

I AM LOOKING FORWARD TO

THREE THINGS THAT MADE ME HAPPY TODAY

TODAY I LEARNED...

A CHALLENGE I OVERCAME

ONE THING I CAN IMPROVE TOMORROW

My Positive Affirmation for Today...

Date:

"PEACE CAN ARRIVE IN VERY SMALL FORMS."
PEANUT

TODAY I AM GRATEFUL FOR

I AM LOOKING FORWARD TO

THREE THINGS THAT MADE ME HAPPY TODAY

TODAY I LEARNED...

A CHALLENGE I OVERCAME

ONE THING I CAN IMPROVE TOMORROW

My Positive Affirmation for Today...

Date: ______________

"HORSES DO NOT REPLAY THE WHOLE PASTURE BEFORE SLEEPING.
THEY EAT,BREATHE, SETTLE,
AND TRUST THE MORNING WILL COME."
PEANUT

TODAY I AM GRATEFUL FOR

I AM LOOKING FORWARD TO

THREE THINGS THAT MADE ME HAPPY TODAY

TODAY I LEARNED...

A CHALLENGE I OVERCAME

ONE THING I CAN IMPROVE TOMORROW

My Positive Affirmation for Today...

Date:

"I CARRY A LITTLE PIECE OF EVERY FRIEND, EVERY LESSON, AND EVERY SOFT PLACE I HAVE EVER KNOWN."

PEANUT

TODAY I AM GRATEFUL FOR

I AM LOOKING FORWARD TO

THREE THINGS THAT MADE ME HAPPY TODAY

TODAY I LEARNED...

A CHALLENGE I OVERCAME

ONE THING I CAN IMPROVE TOMORROW

My Positive Affirmation for Today...

Date:

“STAND IN THE SHADE WHEN YOU NEED TO.”
PEANUT

TODAY I AM GRATEFUL FOR

I AM LOOKING FORWARD TO

THREE THINGS THAT MADE ME HAPPY TODAY

TODAY I LEARNED...

A CHALLENGE I OVERCAME

ONE THING I CAN IMPROVE TOMORROW

My Positive Affirmation for Today...

Date:

**"IF YOU LOOK CLOSELY,
EVEN AN ORDINARY PASTURE
IS OVERFLOWING WITH WONDER."**
PEANUT

TODAY I AM GRATEFUL FOR

I AM LOOKING FORWARD TO

THREE THINGS THAT MADE ME HAPPY TODAY

TODAY I LEARNED...

A CHALLENGE I OVERCAME

ONE THING I CAN IMPROVE TOMORROW

My Positive Affirmation for Today...

Date: ______

"IF ALL YOU DID TODAY WAS KEEP GOING, THAT COUNTS."
PEANUT

TODAY I AM GRATEFUL FOR

I AM LOOKING FORWARD TO

THREE THINGS THAT MADE ME HAPPY TODAY

TODAY I LEARNED...

A CHALLENGE I OVERCAME

ONE THING I CAN IMPROVE TOMORROW

My Positive Affirmation for Today...

Date:

**"ORDINARY DAY,
LET ME NOTICE
WHAT A TREASURE YOU
ARE."**

PEANUT

TODAY I AM GRATEFUL FOR

I AM LOOKING FORWARD TO

THREE THINGS THAT MADE ME HAPPY TODAY

TODAY I LEARNED...

A CHALLENGE I OVERCAME

ONE THING I CAN IMPROVE TOMORROW

My Positive Affirmation for Today...

Date:

"A MINI HORSE NOTICES MORE WHEN THEY STOP LOOKIN FOR DANGER."
PEANUT

TODAY I AM GRATEFUL FOR

I AM LOOKING FORWARD TO

THREE THINGS THAT MADE ME HAPPY TODAY

TODAY I LEARNED...

A CHALLENGE I OVERCAME

ONE THING I CAN IMPROVE TOMORROW

My Positive Affirmation for Today...

Date:

"LET YOUR THOUGHTS BE SOFT PLACES TO STAND."

PEANUT

TODAY I AM GRATEFUL FOR

I AM LOOKING FORWARD TO

THREE THINGS THAT MADE ME HAPPY TODAY

TODAY I LEARNED...

A CHALLENGE I OVERCAME

ONE THING I CAN IMPROVE TOMORROW

My Positive Affirmation for Today...

Date:

"YOUR HEART DOES NOT NEED TO GALLOP TO GET SOMEWHERE GOOD."

PEANUT

TODAY I AM GRATEFUL FOR

I AM LOOKING FORWARD TO

THREE THINGS THAT MADE ME HAPPY TODAY

TODAY I LEARNED...

A CHALLENGE I OVERCAME

ONE THING I CAN IMPROVE TOMORROW

My Positive Affirmation for Today...

Date: ____________

"LET TODAY GIVE YOU ONE THING WORTH KEEPING."
PEANUT

TODAY I AM GRATEFUL FOR

I AM LOOKING FORWARD TO

THREE THINGS THAT MADE ME HAPPY TODAY

TODAY I LEARNED...

A CHALLENGE I OVERCAME

ONE THING I CAN IMPROVE TOMORROW

My Positive Affirmation for Today...

Gratitude
does not mean
the day was easy.

It means
something soft
still found you

PEANUT

Made in the USA
Coppell, TX
28 June 2026

83667788R00056